Beautiful Fire

Beautiful Fire

Joyce Ash

DENVER

SPEARS MEDIA PRESS LLC
Denver
7830 W. Alameda Ave, Suite 103-247 Denver, CO 80226
United States of America

First Published in 2018 by Spears Media Press
www.spearsmedia.com
info@spearsmedia.com
Information on this title: www.spearsmedia.com/beautiful-fire

ISBN: 978-1-942876-25-0 (Paperback)

Also Available in Kindle (ebook)

Spears Media Press has no responsibility for the persistence or accuracy of
urls for external or third-party internet websites referred to in this publication,
and does not guarantee that any content on such websites is, or will remain,
accurate or appropriate.

Book & Cover Design by Spears Media Press
Cover Photograph: (CCO) Pexels.com

To my younger sister, Dr. Helen A. Ashuntantang.
In celebration...!

&

To my friends at the University of Hartford.
Much obliged for your support!

ACKNOWLEDGEMENTS

"Because We Are Poor," and "Speaking Up" previously titled "Splinter in Many Stars" were first published in *Dhaka Anthology of World Poetry*. Ed. Aminur Rahman and Bilkis Monsoor. Dhaka, Bangladesh. Adorn Publishers, 2018

"A Defiant Face" first appeared in *Poems for the Hazara: A Multilingual Poetry Anthology and Collaborative Poem by 125 Poets from 68 Countries*. Ed. Kamran Mir Hazar. New York, USA: Full Page Publishing, 2014.

"Birth-Day" and "Incantation" were first published in *Reflections: An Anthology of New Work by African Women Poets*. Boulder, Colorado: Lynne Rienner Publishers, 2013.

Slight variations of the poems, "Jabulani" "Identity," "Your Son" "Forget-Me-Not" "For Junction Here," "Embers of Coal," and "My Heart Go Burst "first appeared on my blog www.Joyceash.com and/or my Facebook page.

"Jabulani" with a variation on the title, "Jabulani: The World Cup Ball" also published in *Free Verse: A Journal of Contemporary Poetry and Poetics*, Issue 22 (2012).

Some of the poems in this volume like "Jabulani," "Something Remained" "Because We Are Poor," "My New Husband," and "Into the Beautiful Fire" have been performed publicly to vast audiences at poetry festivals in Medellin, Colombia, Athens, Greece and Dhaka Bangladesh.

Contents

Part I: Call Me Woman

Birth-Day

I was asleep son when you came.
You did not see my eyes nor hear my voice.

When I held you son, pain tattooed my body,
And my nipple fumbled in your waiting mouth.

I had no mother by me as should have been,
So no pepper soup to heal my bleeding womb.

How can I tell you son,
The wings of love did not fly at first sight?

That I was an alien in a foreign land
Lost in the thicket of lonely tears?

But Son, in the cushion of my arm
You gulped the prayer from my heart.

Now at 15 questions abound as manhood,
Prances on the edge of the boy.

But some truths you will never know
You were not born with a womb.

Incantation

I sit by her side on a snowy day far from our girly days
When the sun's rays bathed our bodies
And our breasts were just body parts.
Her bald hair doesn't scream "chemo."

She looks like a glamour star,
A cross between O'Connor and Alek Wek.
Pain has purified her body.
Her stories are incantations.

Like her head, her memory is clean;
She tells of that night of seduction
Under cheap lights in a dusty student room.
Her breasts now mangled, were juicy mangoes then.

His hands found them, squeezing them jointly into his mouth.
Beneath him, she danced to "*Nyuwe*,"*
Directing him to the seat of her soul,
But he ate her body and spat out the rest.

That's when the cancer began.
The next morning she tore the picture of cupid
Above her six-spring Vono bed.
No more prayers to foreign gods!

Today pain cuts her breathing
And she talks between gasps.
Tomorrow I will come with a notebook.
Pain knows how to tell
A
True
Story.

*A popular song by Dina Bell, a Cameroonian artist.

Turkish Bath in Fez Morocco

We stood there, naked, facing each other
United in our tabooed body parts,
Enveloped in more than the hot steam
Of a Hammam experience.

No shared language between us
We spoke with our determined spirits.
Her Muslim grey hairs imparting lessons
To my Christian black tufts.

An old woman bathing a grown woman!
Her sponge embarked on a journey,
Cleaning the tough turf of womanhood
Scrubbing dead skin from generations of pain.

I said "Thank you" with a naked wet embrace;
Our breasts touching in renewed faith,
Mocking barriers from a divided world.
I walked out radiant into a blinding sunlight!

Identity

You tell me you did not fall from a tree.
You have a father, and you want his name,
So today you carry a piece of paper with
A new name, a flash light of identity.

They say I am a good woman
Because I do not tell how your father laughed
At the love that brought him into my thighs,
And hung my hymen like a pendant on his neck.

They say I am a real African woman
Because I do not tell of my nine-month agony,
His mother mocking my mother at the market place
Saying his son is no fool to fall for trash like me.

They say my stomach is a guarded store
Because I do not tell you that my brain
Could find x even in the absence of y,
But your father's P made me a "slut" fit for no school.

They say I have the wisdom of a tortoise
Because I allowed your father to drive that big car
Through our family's honor and pain
In exchange for that sought-after visa to a foreign land

They say you must be grateful to me;
I gave up my life for yours to soar.
But my child, a paper is a paper
Your identity is beyond paper! Remember!

Your Son

Yesterday our son was your son alone,
As he made touch downs into your patriarchal heart.
You pranced the sidelines
Showing off the semblance of your nose.
Your chest moving ahead, you said:
"That's my boy."
"He is a chip off the old block."
Today he became my son
Because the police nailed him with ½ a pound of weed.
Today he became my son because no fool like that
 Could have your blood in his veins.
Today he became my son in a cold court house
With papers to sign.
Today he became my son alone
Like when, he was, in my womb!

Next of Kin

He stands before me, not a day taller than my last-born.
A last attempt of our father's quest to find a next of kin.

He stands before me with nothing but his manhood
Buoyed by customs not sanctioned by the times.

He stands before me announcing my breast have drawn the line:
No land or house will carry my name.

I look past him to a sprawling farm of memories;
I turn the earth on each ridge with a familiar hoe.

He can't remember my vaselined fingers
Healing his bloated circumcised penis.

But should remember my blows on the boy
Who stole his school lunch and bullied him.

I look him over, sorry for the boy hiding behind the man
He is my kin, anger evades me. I will pass. Next!

A Libation of Words: For Maya Angelou

Maya Angelou, etangti ngoreh,* still you rise from the ashes of
history!
An ancestral presence, visible to those who feel.
Yes, the earth will not confine you.
You, an Amazon, daughter of the sun, phenomenal woman!
You who straddled the world in body and words;
You who brought healing words to painful spaces.
You who sang courageously from the cage,
Your voice breaking free the hinges of our own cages.
Today we gather in your name, pouring a libation of words.
My people say it best:
"erong ambeu ereuh, erob asem ereuh-reuh."
The past was good; the future will be good too!
May we forever measure our feet
On your oversized footprints

*Strong woman

Questions at the Beginning of Knowing

Tell me about your "friend" in your house.
Are you her friend too, or a yoke around her neck?

Tell me about her walks in the park again
When she walks where does her shadow fall?

Tell me about her showers taken in the dark?
Do the wet arrows pierce or soothe her pores?

What of her sounds in that huge space which could be home?
Does she yelp, moan or groan?

What colors does she like? Deep orange of deceit?
Or shades of green and blue for hope to rise?

I like friends of a friend in a network of friends
Tell me playboy, who else is your friend?

My New Husband

This evening I told my new husband:
I will come to bed by 9 P.M.
To spread the table for a long nightly feast.
I will banish night clothes from my closet;
I will be Eve without the apple,
A human body in his garden
Waiting for a holy harvest.

This evening I told my new husband:
No more travelling to conferences
Seeking knowledge beyond his brain.
My travels will be limited
To where his driving takes me.
Stuck by his side, I will prove
I was taken from his rib.

This evening I told my new husband:
I will waste no time in taking his name,
And tame the urge to self-identify.
As for children, I give up my womb;
He is our kid for life…
But it is 2. A.M.
I realize I am writing another poem!

Ocular Mistake

Ah Othello, your rage whipped me.
You rubbed my honor in mud but I stood tall.
Even now I accuse you not.
Your stories wooed me;
Your trials flayed me.
I married you at the altar of faith,
To prove Venice wrong,
But the Iagos around you
Who are not who they are
Stabbed your naked ego
Till you foamed in the mouth.
Now I'm gone and the curtains fall.

Jabulani*

A man is like a jabulani, the world cup ball.
In a woman's arms he jerks in spasms.

Drowned in the moans of any vuvuzela,
He does "the Robert Green"** and slips inside.

Hard to contain, a jabulani flies
To arms of fans in stands,

Defying poise, skill and control
Or corner kicks from yearning hearts.

It is not a question of referees
Or countless replays on a wide screen.

Some women already know what Adidas knows:
A jabulani is a jabulani!

Even the best sometimes miss.
After all, every net has its holes!

*The official 2010 FIFA world cup ball heavily criticized for being too light weight and impossible to control.

** English Goalkeeper at the 2010 world cup ridiculed for "spilling" a ball which rolled over the goal line into the net.

Blunt

I don't want to write poetry.
No mix of metaphors here.
Whether direct or indirect.
No similes to compare anything.
I will tell you this: straight up.
SEX is a toy;
Sex is an end.
There's no gentleman between his legs!

Your white dress is part of the act.
You're playing virgin, for you are not.
Once in the drama you stay right inside,
Playing his mama, his sister even his mistress.
There's nothing like "becoming one,"
If he dies you learn the truth.
In some parts, you "belonged to him"
Counted and disposed like property.

Don't give me no crap about love.
Your best friend is your plastic,
And non-alkaline batteries.
Pick your shape, pick your color.
You need no babble in your ear,
And no heap of snoring sounds,
So this is it. I said it.
Blunt! Blunt! Blunt!

Something Remained

For all pregnant women who die from abuse and those living with the scars

I want to write a poem in anger,
But I am no poet, only a woman with a womb,
A witness to my sister's pain.
Her dying sounds finding my beleaguered ear:
"Not for me, not just for me
Leave me to breathe life in this sacred shrine."

But Blood stains opened a path for her.
Her womb ran on legs of faith.
Violent steps encircled her light;
Other body parts struggled for life,
And death gathered them all in its hands
Except her womb, slippery with life.

She's gone now, but her bloody stains
Scream on the sleeves of your shirt.
They cry in the armpits of your public face,
And Flowers of her agony sprout in your sleep.
No one wrestles with a God and wins;
Every woman with a womb is a God!

A Divine Bond

For Brandi, surrogate mom on Mother's Day 2017

You would never know all of us
From Italy to Cameroon, the world over.
You may never hear the noise of our joy
Bursting the plastic of helpless phones.
You may never see the twinkle in our eyes
As we gush at the miracle you carried;
The halo of your sublime gift
Circles our hearts and minds.
Today, we bring our basket of thanks,
For you our mother-angel;
Just a little token for our spring blossom.
Nothing will ever match your selfless grace.
Tomorrow we will still exclaim
And always remember your name.
How else are we to respond?
Your womb is our divine bond.

The Eagle's Iroko

For Professor (Mrs.) Christie Okoli Achebe on hearing of the death of her husband, Chinua Achebe

Tufia Kwa! She will not be in the ashes
We the *Umuada* of Achebe's world have spoken.

On both sides of the Atlantic we come
To dry her tears with slices of the sun.

She who put a heart in the writer's chest,
To steady his soul on our shifting earth.

She who received Chinua's lone bribe
No Longer At Ease "for Christie Okoli."

She who took his bait, putting him at ease
And stayed at her post till the very end.

She who planted her feet on the ground like roots
A sturdy iroko for the celebrated Eagle.

No, the color of mourning will not touch her skin.
We bring *okwuma** to nourish her feet.

Life is for the living; day wipes out night.
It is another morning on creation day!

*Shea butter

Notes

I miss Waikiki, Honolulu.
The breeze rushing through
Hawaiian palms;
The waves traveling at sea towards me.
The smiling faces drenched
In aloha spirit.
But…
What I miss most…
Are your notes under my door!
"Could we meet at 6 for dinner?
"Could we share a cab tonight?"
My spirit still answers "yes."

My Piece of Glass

For Lynn Pasquerella

I just came in and you are leaving.
I don't complain, for you left me with a gift.

You cracked that glass ceiling again;
Its pieces scatter about me.

I have picked one up and wiping it clean,
I see my face and my own potential.

There's no other gift from one woman to another,
Than the gift of doing and showing.

Tomorrow around the camp fire
With little girls looking at me

I'll tell the story of the provost
A woman, born of woman

Intelligent, calm and focused
The 18th president of her alma mater.

I will tell them, I came in and she left,
Leaving my feet planted on solid earth.

Speaking Up

For Koumate Monique, 31

Three days now and you will not leave me.
Your blood spills on the streets of my mind,
Dripping slowly inside my humane chambers.
What world kills a woman many times over?

Your pregnant body lying in public shames our eyes.
Your children inside gasping for air demand action.
My tears frozen in shock hang stiff, so stiff;
What world kills a woman many times over?

A woman hunched over you ignites my soul.
A true Amazon of our times determined to save lives.
Her courage mocks my visible silence!
What world kills a woman many times over?

They say the dead can hear and see.
Do you see me hunched over your story?
Vowing your life will splinter into many stars?
My silence will not kill you again!

The Elevator of Your Smile

For Ida Schaechter who died during the Connecticut blackout of 2011

I rode the elevator of your smile each morning,
Adjusting my sight on the rims of your glasses.
Your questions found their answers in my body's laughter,
But I did not know your name.

I measured my future by your spritely gait,
Balancing my hips on your staircase of grace.
I saw my future in your morning grin,
But I did not know your name.

I waved the tea of my earth into your empty cup,
Forcing your honest words like dew drops.
"I want to drink what my stomach knows."
But I did not know your name.

Death, bold and brazen, named you for me.
In the elevator of your spirit I'm now locked,
Interrogating and probing. Which is better?
To know your smile or your name?

A Poem from My Son's Eyes

I love it when my mother comes
To my room and sits beside me;
Her bubbly laughter rocking the air.
Our teenage stories merging,
Linking history and the stormy present.
I learn; I laugh and laugh,
Rocking my body from side to side
Eyes glistening in their boyish sockets.
I manage to ask one question:
"Is every mother like this?"

Bring Back Our Girls

For Chibok girls, 2014

I can't forget you all even in the frenzy of the world cup
Your hearts leap in my dreams choking my breath

I see your eyes in the young girls around me
Even as I kiss goodnight to my sons at night

Images of your parents' agony torment my day
Affecting the taste of food on my tongue

How do your fathers sleep at night?
Grown men with captive daughters rendered helpless?

All we have been left with are mere words,
"Bring back our girls," hoping for magic!

Water na Life: A Poem in Cameroon Pidgin English

Ma grand pikin na school dat don start.
I say make I talk small talk, give you too goo- luck.
Di white-man kontri fine but...
When ya mami be dey ya age na puff-puff for morning
When ma hand be fit reach.
Motor no be dey, na foot-foot for reach school.
For here chop plenty too much;
Na beg we di beg before you gree for chop.
For here bus di take you go; ih bring you back.
Plenti talk dey for ma heart ma pikin.
Ya mami don learn plenti book, ya papa too.
Book fine; ih don give dem money.
But ting wey I want make you learn
Na for get heart for people.
When morning reach salot ya mami; salot ya papa;
Find side way me too adey, whether I wake-up for sleep.
When ya mami talk, hear first before you answer.
Book na fine ting but fashion di gi long life.
Na water dis I di troway for ya foot
All place wey you enter; you go comot fine.
Water na life!

Innocence in Nicaragua

He must have been nine going on ten.
His outstretched hand right in my face.
Bright eyed, dimpled laughter, then
His tiny voice asking to embrace.

I wear his innocence like a cloak.
My hands finding his to dance;
Laughing and framing it a joke. But
He wiggled like he was in a trance.

His smiles trap my maternal heart;
How do young boys learn the ways of men?
His tiny fingers set mine apart.
My dancing steps question; then

He drops his hairless back on the floor;
Inviting my pulsing hips on his crutch.
I pause my steps; surprised to the core.
His innocence was palpable to touch.

Part II: Nuggets of Passion

Into The Beautiful Fire

I want to come to the forge with you,
To see you fashion a new life for me.

The tongues of fire licking warm
Juice from the pores of my body.

I want to come to the forge with you
To see your flaming hands sculpt words

That travel from my navel disappearing
In that abyss of bliss hidden from sight.

Let me faint at your feet in that forge,
And feel your mouth breathe life from your rivers.

Pray, let me come to the forge with you,
Measure my sweat with the goblet of your heart.

Poetry in the Bedroom

I don't want my poetry in the classroom;
I want it in the bedroom
Where the body breathes through its pores,
And eyes do not begrudge the tongue its luck.
I want it in the bedroom where soft colored blinds
Guard unscripted bodies, and
Echo songs from unguarded lips.
Keep my poetry in the bedroom, a fuel
At dawn when legs untangle to face the rising sun.
Take poets to the classroom;
Leave my poems between sheets.

A Digital Moment

After so long, I am finally in your
Digital presence. Seeing is believing!

You unbutton my blouse with your eyelids.
My nipples stare at your brown manly chest.

Your passionate gaze forces my lips apart
Like a helpless fish on a sandy shore.

You rise in front of my very own eyes
Standing tall and nodding in admiration.

I twist and turn on the rhythm of my pulse
Doing my choreography of desire.

Any moment now the screen will give way...
It's been so long in coming; Oh so long!

The Pulse of Love

Looking at you in the glow of lights
My body burns for your cooling fires.
How can I contain the waves building inside?

I squeeze you gently on the dance floor
Like I'm testing the ripeness of a mango.
How do I stop this hunger burning my lips?

Your slit reveals a scar known to my eyes;
My fingers long to touch and make you squirt.
How do I stop this bulge sprouting here?

Memory on memory fuels my aching desire
Threading from agape days of childhood.
How do I prove my love beyond this lust?

In the Bookstore

Let me be that book in your hand. Enjoying
Your intent gaze shutting out all else;
Your fingers turning each page tenderly.
Your feet rooted in awe on one spot.

Oh to be the pages you thumb daily,
Or the letters on the pages you read.
Then your eyes would lock me
In that warm quiet embrace I see.

How I want to feed your eager eyes,
So you can take me home with you;
Bookmarking my tender spots,
Returning each day to me with desire.

A Song for Two

Come to me my Love!
Let us show the world how love happens
Crossing human borders and walls.
Surrender your hand in mine;
Feel my rhythmic squeeze
Slow, steady like Dhaka traffic.
Experience the pulse of my desire!

Take my hand my love
Feel the warmth of my blood rising.
Look into my eyes;
See my human hunger.
Taste my sweetness in your spirit.
Wet me with the waters of your Nile;
Circle my life with new light!

Lady's Slipper

Life's design is an unpredictable art
Looking at the path my heart is charting.
Here I am cradling your heart in my palm!
Did you say we'll talk later?

Your last words often catch me off guard
Never ready for another anxious separation.
My pulse quickening into a known rhythm,
The meek sound of my passionate blues.

If only I was like a "touch me not"
Closing up quickly after every touch,
But your words leave me,
Like a 'Lady's slipper,' open and waiting.

Cigarette

I want to be a cigarette,
If only to touch your lips,
Feel the wetness of your mouth,
Lie on your tongue,
Burn with desire,
Turn soft
Into ash!

Embers of Coal

Some things refuse to go the way of all things
Like you reaching out to say "hello,"
Arriving each time like expected rain,
Watering the dry riverbed of memories.

We squash distances at a button's touch.
In the warmth of your virtual breath,
We lounge in the mutual longings of time
 Pushing the frontiers of our being.

What does it matter where you are?
Who measures the taste of honey
On longing tongues, or firmness of
A nipple in a child's waiting mouth?

In the mirror's reflection I see my eyes
A harvest of questions blinking,
Yet the embers of coal remain hot
Waiting and wanting your whiff of wind.

Message from Buea-Bamenda-Mamfe

Your silence was no alarm song stealing dreams from my sleep.
The blood on the streets was your letter to me.

The enraged masses became your email;
The dreams on placards twitted your desires...

You are the elephant who comes at the rear of the herd;
You are the farmer who fends off birds from your neighbor's
farm.

Aneh nta ya*, I never looked through the door for your shadow.
No true warrior sleeps on his bed when the drums of war disturb
our peace.

You belong to the people; I, a servant of the gods
Till the soil where you plant your feet and feed your soul.

*Beloved

Forget-Me-Not

When I was a child I measured my steps
With bright flowers on the narrow
Shortcuts to school. Two flowers I still remember:
The sunflower at the start of my journey.
It's petals like the sun lit my way
I touched it not for fear I would delay.

But for every forget-me-not
I stopped and picked a bunch.
They were near my journey's end.
The white, blue and purple
Always seduced my youthful eyes.
I rubbed them on my sweaty nose,
And brushed them softly against my lips.

Many years have gone by, but
There's something I want you to know:
Each time you rub your nose against mine,
And part my lips so softly,
My soul whispers tenderly…
"Forget-me-not."

For Junction Here: A Poem in Cameroon Pidgin English

Whenever I shidon for this place
All ting wey I di see na your face.
Na for this junction I be used to see
your heart; As I be want make we be.

You no be ever gree me I touch you;
Your own konto be too much.
I go beg; look you with water for my eye.
Tell you say all ting na for try.

But for this junction you no be fit pretend.
Na for this place we be di end.
You take your road go; I waka go my own.
Na for this place; this very place.

That time your eye di remain for down.
Your right hand di play with your gown.
Your one foot di dig dust; way for go no dey;
Your eye di weak; your heart want stay.

Today, Junction off license na ma place.
Any evening I buy one man cold my heart.
Na only you know say no bi mimbo I want;
Na you I di still find, for junction here!

Before the Surgery

Looking forward cements hope.
Wiser truths hash on yesterdays.

Looking forward clears the dew;
Wetting paths; firming steps.

Looking forward conjures faith;
Leaving wholeness in its stead.

"Looking forward..." Remember?
That's all you said; for me, it was enough.

Where Are You?

Maybe we move nearer nirvana this way,
When I chase you then you chase me and I chase you.

Maybe you can only find my G-spots after they
Are swollen with desire from induced absences.

Maybe it is a game of chance after all!
We hide; we seek; we find!

Do You Pray at Night?

She stands alone in the center of your palm
Doing a ballet of life unrehearsed.
You laugh and laugh;
Each throaty laugh
Caressing her supple lips.
Your half sighs in between
Entangling her half dreams.
Then one random question:
Do you pray at night?
She answers softly,
"No, I love you,
Prayer-fully
Trapped between night and day."

A Pretty Good Game

Since you've been gone she has not played.
Her toy sits lonely- almost forgotten.
Wrapped in sheets of nostalgia it waits,
Hungry for her friendly hands and your gaze.

Maybe she's too old for games now. But
When she sees your face in the mirror
The woman in her remembers your voice:
"Where is your toy?" "Go bring your toy."

Passionate obedience drives her memory.
Your seductive gaze gives rhythm to her hands.
She welcomes it in the warmth of her body.
No one outgrows a pretty good game!

Texting

ILU for I love you.
Ruf2t for «Are you free tonight?»
What are these?
Where are the words in their glory?
Full and long?
Words that fill the mouth
Touching the roof of desires?
Like a tongue picking the crevices for dripping juice.
Full words sweep the corners of forgotten dreams.
Find them; bring them.
When you text
Make it full, keep it long
Long is good!

Letter to a Poet

Dear Poet
Your words squeeze my balls;
Rub honey on my pole.
When you put simple words in strange places
You place my dick in strange cunts
A fantasy I foolishly crave.
Your words are my lover,
I pine for their return
Holding shadows at dawn.
Just your words
Nothing more!

Delirium

Tonight I will be at the airport to bid you farewell;
You will squeeze my hand discreetly.
When hands slowly untangle,
You will utter deep-seated words
Filling my basket of desired memories.
Later, I will unpack your words
Hanging them on lines of sunny recall.
But today is still young,
Burning the weight of waiting on my skin.
The airport is in my body, delirious
With your impending "goodbye."

Imperfection

There's something beautiful about imperfection;
It never claims to be that which it is not,
Like flowers blooming from an ice bucket
Instead of a flower vase,
Like crumpled sheets bearing witness
To a sweet sinful "yes."
Like knowing we are still God's children,
Naked. Imperfect...

Part III: Politics of Being

Because We Are Poor…

They rule and rule and we cannot talk.
When we cry "democracy,"
Dem-go-crazy,
And stuff our mouths with stolen ballots.
We eat till we puke.

Because we are poor!

We fall for "free,"
And land empty handed on our butt.
Nothing free carries a spine.
On fours we crawl and scratch the earth.

Because we are poor!

They always find new slaves
To bring a Babel of tongues.
New slaves with their sheathed tongues.
Shameless models for their new posters.

Because we are poor!

The houseboy steals and brings the loot home.
A new chief with humble roots;
Close enough to steal from his own.
His stained smile a marked betrayal.

Because they made us poor!

They woo us in our own homes
Bringing kola nuts of their guilt,
But wo/man does not live by kola nut alone,
But on every drop of ancestral blood.

Because we have *never been poor!*

Ma Heart go Burst! : A Poem in Cameroon Pidgin English

After the Yaoundé-Douala Highway Road collapse and train accident at Eseka in Cameroon on 10/21/16

Weh' eh! na which kind trouble meet'up we so eh?
Na which god or ngambe fit fix this one?
For one day road go broke, train too capsize?
Ma heart go burst for this place wey I shidon so.

Sorry-picture dem dong gump for ma heart,
People way dem die oh; people way body broke oh,
Small pikin oh, big person oh, all chakara outside.
Ma heart go burst for this place wey I shidon so.

Person wey ih sey make dem add train long sotey,
Da person go ih own school na for wusai noh?
Na which kind loss-sense that for day time?
Ma heart go burst for this place wey I shidon so.

Big man dong enter country like actor.
Ih gi command here; ih gi command there.
Wusai ih been dey wey road old sotey ih broke?
Ma heart go burst for this place way I shidon so.

Today, all ting di waka for hospital for seka accident.
So doctor dem be fit work so eh?
So government be fit gi free merecine so eh?

Ma heart go burst for this place wey I shidon so.

Ah ma country! Ih go hard for move heart for you
Ih go hard for me for see ya trouble I no shake
We di sing'am for anthem, but I mean'am for ma heart
"And deep endearment forever more"*

*Last line of the chorus of the Cameroon National Anthem in English.

The Children of the Hearth Have Come

For Anglophone Cameroon Youths

The Children of the hearth have come.
They have come to reclaim their future.
Their footprints find their marching pair in the dust laden
Debris of an almost forgotten story.

They march inside the mansion of their history
Opening windows into neglected spaces.
Laughing ghosts in chambers of memory
Haunt and mock their indolent present.

Refrain: The children of the hearth have come!

They saunter into the kitchen of hidden desires
Sweeping ashes from fires long extinguished.
Faithful stones of the fireplace re-pay
The debt of stories which must be told.

They follow blood stains into secret vaults;
There Abendong lies, frozen at 24.
His life drowned in myths by innocent children.
His death will be their death if they dare forget.

Refrain: The children of the hearth have come!

They scour the living rooms of yesterday
flipping through albums of betrayed dreams.
Trapped flashes illuminate frozen images
of ancestors waiting for an overdue libation.

Refrain: The children of the hearth have come.

At the Martyrs' Monument, Dhaka

For my people in Cameroon after the tragic events on October 1, 2017

I know you can guess what was on my mind
Facing heroes at martyrs' place in Savar on that Dhaka road,
Martyrs of a nine month scorch
From March to December 1971.

I know you can guess what I said
When I heard how the oppressor was ruthless,
3 million killed dying for a new land to emerge:
Bangladesh! No more East Pakistan.

I know you felt my chest rise
When I heard of villages burned,
Young men, women and children killed;
Their blood crying loud for a new day.

I know you saw my tears among planted trees
Walking in the footprints of history,
Hoping, dreaming praying, wanting.
Every heart needs a real home.

I know you heard my voice in defiance:
"Nothing lasts forever, nothing,"
Walking slowly, steadily
From that sacred martyrs' place in Dhaka!

The Day the President Will Fall

The day the President will fall,
Four decades of my nightmare
Will finally end with the dawn
Of my beautiful teenage hopes.

The day the President will fall,
The cataracts of greed that blinded some
Will fall; forcing them to see the pain
And misery of people next door.

The day the President will fall,
Those abusing government coffers will fall.
Their senile servitude and thievery
No longer supporting their bloated egos.

The day the President will fall,
May it not be an elephant's fall.
Blighting the land with its weight
And putrid stench of rotting carcass.

One Death Is Too Many

A Villanelle for Kurds in Afrin City

How many deaths are considered too many?
The answer drips in ink from every clime.
No one can kill the healing words of poets.

Human fragments claim abandoned fields.
Villages lay bare murders most foul.
How many deaths are really considered too many?

Cries from Afrin echo in chambers of bleeding hearts.
I write for them with ink flowing from my soul.
No one can kill the healing words of poets.

Tears demand answers from terrified eyes;
Mothers bury pain in shallow innocent graves.
How many deaths are really considered too many?

Tomorrow begs to be born in a rainbow of hope.
Poets rally for a new rousing immortal song.
No one can kill the healing words of poets.

And when they kill Kurds like they do small ants.
Witness our voices converge in global protest:
One death is indeed way too many.
O spread these healing words of poets.

A Defiant Face

A Poem for Hazara People

Near Siah Chob Village
Your face sings a defiant song:
Hazara! Hazara! Hazara!
And the refrain echoes in octaves
From Khawat through Chardeh,
From Mirasi Valley to Banyam.
Your mismatched shoes are
The arrows for the tiny bows.
No one can steal your sun.
No winter can cheat your dreams.
For the waters of Lazir River.
Have found my flaming pen.
I may never know your name,
But the language of your face,
Is my grenade on their parade!

Behind the Laughter

Behind the laughter are pages of life
With pain etched in red ink;
Others with tears that embrace the day.
Pages with impulses sitting on edge

Behind the laughter are flowers of faith.
The hibiscus of childhood.
The rose of adolescence.
The carnations of exile.

Behind the laughter are passions of time,
Teasing tales from the hands of the clock,
Counting the sand in the hour glass;
Waiting for the cattle egrets to return.

I Don't Make Lemonade

When life gives me lemons
I don't make lemonade.
I hold them in my hands,
Look at them
Lovingly…deeply… I say:

Behold, these are lemons!
My eyes drink in
Their fine sunny color.
Their skin evenly rough to the touch
Revives the nerves in my palms.

Their pointed nipple tips
Tickle the edges of my nose;
I breathe in the healing fragrance.
I cut the lemons open;
Their tangy taste wakes up my insides.

Alert, I engage life, face-to-face,
Energized, healed and renewed.
Lemonade is an added luxury;
When life gives me lemons
I enjoy them in their own right!

Shiny Stones

After watching the rescue of 33 Chilean miners on TV on 10/13/10

They each descended to search for
Shiny stones
To feed the maggots of our capitalist greed.
They got lost in the abyss of our fleshy desires.
Buried for 69 days they did not see gold
But toxic dust from incessant rocks.
Now caged in the womb of the phoenix
They're reborn
One,
After one,
After one.
Their eyes wear shades.
Truth is blinding!

PiTY

Don't push me into
A well full of PiTY.
You can't nail my dreams on the arms of T,
Or wrap my emotions around the tail of Y.
Yes, I refuse to sink; I refuse to drown.
I stand up like P, pushing upward.
I am rising still…upward, upward.
I have taken off
Like the dot above i!

The Pilot

His blackness caught my eyes;
His sinewy body challenged my lust.
My thoughts dressed him in a Sanja*
Settled him in Ashum village,
A horn of palm wine in hand.
But we were in a plane, ready for take-off.
From the cockpit his voice twirled
"This is your Captain speaking…"
His Jamaican accent inflamed my pride;
My smile dangled on ashes of colonialism.
He announced he was in charge;
He will get us there on time. Then,
Memories of the graveyard in the Atlantic
And years of "white only" signs
Lynch my smile on the trees of our minds.
I breathe deep determined to believe him.

*Traditional loincloth attire.

Seeds of Support

For Ndedi Eyango in 2014

I replant these seeds of support from your vast harvest.
Let them sprout in moments of your need.
The same way you have done for me, for us.
You have always been there in words, in song:
When we were misunderstood- *ma vie est devenue une histoire…*
When life manhandled our dreams –*Chacun a des problem ..Alima eh*
When we loved far away from home - *L'amour n'a pas de couleur*
When we needed to remember our roots -*Mseka Folk…*
When we were frustrated with love- *You must calculer…*
When we interfered wrongly in love, *Between man and woman*
When we had to face a sudden change -*On tourne la Page…*
When death camped at our door steps - *a Kwedi oh…*
When we had to learn to love again - *l'école de l'amour…*
When we missed the land of our birth- *Nkongsamba …*
Yes, I return to you your own seeds planted over time.
Seeds that blossomed even in distant climes.
I plant them now in your own soil.
Let them sprout courage!
Let them sprout wisdom!
Let them sprout faith!
Remain standing
Like the mountain. You,
Our Prince of the Mountain!

Life

Ageing is a long quiet song in body spaces.
The acid refluxing its way to the chest;
The bathroom breaks in the middle of shows.
The slow movement to the twilight zone.

The rhythmic strains pulsate the body too.
Maturity is a known aphrodisiac.
Bodies entwined in deliberate symphony.
Who fears the gates of hell at this age?

My people say "Nɛ rɔŋ apú mbɔ nɛ tuo"*
A baby's cry is anxiously awaited;
But sounds of our exit nag and tug.
Listen, sing-along, play-along. Life!

*The way we leave differs from the way we enter.

Harvest of Light

For Hillyer College, University of Hartford. In Celebration of the Opening of the Shaw Center, September 13, 2013

Lead:
I pour a libation of words for these walls.
The past was good, the present is still good.
If walls could speak these walls will tell
Of the foundation of dreams where they plant their feet.
The pillars of sacrifice holding them up to a slice of the sun,
But we who live here know the language of walls
And so we have come with drops of words.
To honor you, Hillyer's past and present, teachers, mentors, friends.

Response:

Today we celebrate this harvest of light
Like birds on a wing, longing!
We perch on your dreams planted on a soil of faith.
Your light shines, your light leads.
We have answered your call to light.

Lead:
For those gone ahead, our hearts flood their banks.
Dean Meinke, Founder of foundations
Yours is a tap root going deep - a source for other roots.
John Roderick, English Chair and poet
Like an ancestor you came with us.
Your books refusing to die; we still keep your shells.
You who planted word after word even in seasons of drought.
Prof. Marilyn Smith, Philosopher and Chair extraordinaire.
And many more whose names tug at our heartstrings!

Response
We pour a libation of thanks.
A guinea fowl hides her treasures from sight;
You were no guinea fowl.
You left your dreams here, your twigs of ideas here.
We are the reapers in the fields of your harvest.

Lead:
Like branches of light the living are here too.
We catch a star on their brow.
Their oversized footprints contain our feet.
Like birds on a fruitful tree we fly their names from our beaks:
Jay and Debbie Shaw, J. Holden Camp; Sandra and Bill Katz;
Keith Larit; Richard Lugli;
S. Edward Weinswig; Floyd Fisher, and many other stars of light.

Response
We pour a libation of thanks.
A guinea fowl hides her treasures from sight.
You are no guinea fowl;
You left your dreams here, your twigs of ideas here.
We are the reapers in the fields of your harvest.

Lead
And so we pour libation teasing the future.
We have watered the road ahead.
May we never tread on scorching earth.

…these words spoken…these words written…
May they steady our feet as we walk within these walls
Built on solid dreams of the past…made golden in this present
By Dean David Goldenberg.

No One Can Tell Me You Are Gone

For Prof. Frank Dello Iocono who died on 2/20/2014

No one can tell me you are gone;
Your smile still hangs on the pathway
Right between CCC building and Hillyer College.
Your voice still traps my footsteps brazing this unending cold.

I still laugh my same loud laughter
At that same junction of our informal ritual
Where you always asked about my day
With no time for me to moan about the winter.

Your jacket swishing always, as you picked your way
Taking your math brain to a waiting classroom,
Just as your words radiated warmth
Leaving remnants of laughter in my eyes.

Forgive me for staying at the bridge
Of the summer bridge program.
My entry point into your wardrobe of sneakers;
My initiation into your genial nature.

It will never be a goodbye from me Frank
Your ancestral presence now inhabits this space
Your nuggets of wisdom have multiplied here
No teacher of your ilk ever dies!

That May Term

I walked the dim corridors of minority discourse;
My life punctuated by the yearning of five students
Wading through the muddy waters of "the other."
Between them and the margins of history
You were an open door,
An oasis on a deserted campus.
The sun's fingers grabbed me at your door
Transfixed on the loamy soil of your smile.
My question was always the same:
Is your door open all year round?

Bad Luck From London

After many strenuous searching days,
Friday delivered a feast for two weary legs.

A vacant house in the summer of 1968.
The address: 13 Forth Bridge Road.

It was not Soyinka's "Telephone Conversation."
No anxious landlord saw the blackness of callers.

She chalked it down to the ways of a Christian God
The story as I quietly recall.

For four long years her heart sang songs of praise
For this Urhobo landlord, a brother in a foreign land.

She was not aware of white superstition;
13 is no lucky number; she learned after the fact.

Now she stops at every ancestral stream
To wash off bad luck brought from London.

Dream

The pain of memory scourged her grieving body;
Voices from the past needled her pensive present.

Their images danced in the evening shadows
Smiling, they winked and faded slowly away.

No one saw the visible glimmer in her eyes
Daring the nightmarish sun escaping the sky.

No one felt the growing calmness in her soul
Mocking the pale depressing moon.

Pain has a way of washing the eyes
Like an Obasinjom, she could see clearly now.

Two shadows, the female paving the way
The male, guarding the rear.

In between she found hallowed ground.
The future is safe. Cheers to life!

A Rose in Athens

You ask me about this rose in Athens,
But my answer may take a whole evening of story-telling.
Egba?*
Ndere!
Egba?
Ndere!
I begin with the seller,
The one who balanced his will on a tray of stemmed roses.
With an immigrant's faith he dangled one rose
Beseeching love to stretch a hand.
And provide a token weekly rent
How was he to know that these poets
Had drained their pens and keyboards of love?
How was he to know that all they had left
Were eyes weaving words in light?
Silence bounced off the empty plates of desserts,
But there was one poet...buoyed by experience
From the ancient sands of Istanbul.
He had learned some things in the chaos of life:
 "Your beloved should be worn out from being kissed
And you should drop exhausted from the smelling of a flower"**
He stretched his hand and bought a rose.
It found a home in my hand.
I am exhausted from the "smelling of a flower."

*A traditional way of beginning a storytelling/riddle session among the Kenyang speaking people of Manyu Division, Cameroon.

**A quote from *There's something I Have Learned from What I've Lived,* a poem by Turkish Poet, Ataol Behramoglu published in his collection of the same title.

When I Was Ten

For Emilia Bechem Ashuntantang

When I was ten I could not have known
It was our last stand as a full family
That six kids would become five.
How was I to know that her life
Would end at 13…
The day she broke that limb
I carried her like a knapsack
Throwing her down when my
Feeble limbs tired out.
Our father frustrated, blurted
"Serves you right"
As her leg hung in the air
Above her hospital bed.
It was the fourth limb to break.
Our father too did not know
Her life would end at 13
With no more lessons to learn.

When the news of her death came
Women in muffled tones
Said they had known:
No ordinary child could
Leave such footprints in our mud:
Beating old men in storytelling contests;
Coming first in class year in, year out.
Her gender too was a sign:
No girl child was so strong
Like a boy,
Hanging on tiny branches
Like a boy.

Playing all sports
Like a boy,
Winning every fight
Like a boy.
But I could not have known
I was only ten.
Now each year
I measure my feet
In her sun-dried
Footprints!

Tantrum

There's only one word
For the way you left.
The look in your eyes.
The sudden movement.
You banged the door;
Opened it again.
Only one word:
TANTRUM!

ABOUT THE AUTHOR

Dr. Joyce Ash is a poet, actress, creative writer and Associate Professor of English at the University of Hartford, Connecticut. She has appeared as an invited poet in many countries around the world, including England, Germany, Nicaragua, Greece, Costa Rica, Colombia, Bangladesh, Cameroon and USA. Her first book of poetry, *A Basket of Flaming Ashes*, was published to great acclaim. She has also contributed to several international anthologies of poetry, including *Dhaka Anthology of World Poetry, Reflections: An Anthology of New Work by African Women Poets, We Have Crossed Many Rivers: New Poetry from Africa and World Poetry Almanac 2011*. A graduate of schools on three continents, Dr. Ash received a BA in English with a minor in Theater Arts from the University of Yaoundé Cameroon; a Master's in Library and Information Science from the University of Aberystwyth, UK; and a PhD in English/ African Literature from the City University of New York. Her poems have been translated into Spanish, Greek, Hebrew, Turkish and Bengali (Bangla).

Printed in the United States
By Bookmasters